Lead the Way to Success!

You are the #1 motivator of your team.
Use the ideas in this book to keep the
momentum going all year long.

The Contests & Awards Team

101
RECOGNITION
Secrets

**Tools for Motivating and
Recognizing Today's Workforce**

ROSALIND JEFFRIES

Performance Enhancement Group Publishing
Bethesda, Maryland
www.recognitionsecrets.com

PEG Publishing
Bethesda, MD

Ordering information:

Quantity Sales: Special discounts are available on quantity purchases by corporations, associations and others. For details, contact the Customer Service Department through www.recognitionsecrets.com or by calling 301-656-4600.

Orders by U.S. trade bookstores and wholesalers: Please contact Sales and Marketing at the above address or telephone number.

Jeffries, Rosalind
    101 recognition secrets: tools for motivating and recognizing today's workforce/Rosalind Jeffries.–2nd edition
    p.c.m.
    ISBN: 0-9648444-4-3

1. Management.   2. Motivation.   3. Title.

Cover design by York Graphic Services Co.
Interior design by Nancy McKeithen

Printed in the United States of America
10 9 8 7 6 5 4

Dedication

This book would not have been possible without the thousands of employees from across the United States and abroad who have shared their stories with me and given me the inspiration and content for this book.

My greatest hopes are that these "secrets" become a way of life for the managers for whom you work, that your workplace becomes a place you look forward to going to each day, and that each of your accomplishments is acknowledged along the way.

Table of Contents

Part III: A Practitioner's Guide — Four Steps to Effective Recognition 93

Foreword

Little acts of kindness go a long way. Whether in the workplace or at home, people will go the extra mile when they feel appreciated. Yet, with the day-to-day stresses in most businesses, many of us fail to incorporate these little acts of appreciation as part of our daily management practices. A while back, I discovered the obvious—even in environments where employee-based values are extolled and substantial efforts are made to put them into practice, there is always a lot more to do, and learn. This book makes the obvious even more so. *101 Recognition Secrets* is all about business and organizations directly benefitting from employees' good deeds. But it is also about employers benefitting indirectly when people display sensitivity to the needs of others, both inside and outside the organization.

These acts make us human, and valuable ones at that. The "secrets" in this book are as basic and elemental as fresh air.

They are common sense in nature—coming in the midst of an academic blitz of new insights in the science of the management process and better pathways to the "effective organization." That's what makes the book so meaningful. It gives fingertip access to simple recognition techniques that can be easily implemented in your day-to-day routines.

101 Recognition Secrets takes only a few minutes to read, and it is worth each and every nanosecond! You can put elements of it to work immediately after reading it, and I hope you will.

The goal of this book is to spread the word that *Recognition is an Important Part of Good Management Practices.* I highly recommend that you add this book to the front end of your management training programs. We did, and our managers are already getting a lot of mileage out of the suggestions it offers.

Robert Holland, Jr.
Former CEO, Ben & Jerry's Homemade, Inc.

Some organizations are still looking for the magic quick fix, but the magic is really in the simplicity of managing people well.

*We're talking about the same thing we all say
to the people in our lives:
"I want to know that you value me."*

Introduction

Since 1983, I have listened to employees describe how starved they are for a simple "thank-you." I became so frustrated with management's lack of regard for their employees' contributions that I took on the battle, and have continued to write, lecture, and teach about the subject of employee recognition for the past 20 years.

The first edition of *101 Recognition Secrets* provided simple, quick, practical tools for recognition. Since its publication, I have read hundreds of exit interview forms, reviewed employee satisfaction survey results, taught thousands of managers about recognition, and listened to employees cry out for a pat on the back. Through all that, I didn't see enough employee recognition. I did see managers who are eager to learn more about the concept, and I realized that the basics of this critical management skill were missing from the first book.

This edition of *101 Recognition Secrets* teaches managers how to gather employee data, how to link recognition to their everyday operations, and how to put recognition to work every day.

We are now in the new millennium, but we continue to see statistics like Gallup's recent poll showing that only 38% of employees are completely satisfied with the amount of recognition they get for their accomplishments. Why? Because while organizations continue to spend billions of dollars on leadership and management training each year, they overlook the importance of recognition as a key management competency. And because, when asked why they are not taking the time to acknowledge their work-force, managers continue to offer excuses, excuses, excuses.

All employees believe that they are competent—sometimes brilliant—in their work, and that their contributions have value. But they need to *hear* it. In my 20 years of "crusading," I've frequently heard comments like this: "We just want to be noticed for our contributions on a day-to-day basis!"

In short, people want more individual recognition for their performance. From our research of more than 25,000 managers and employees over the past six years, we know that inadequate recognition, rather than insufficient compensation, is the most common reason employees give for quitting.

When we take performance for granted and do not recognize individuals on a regular basis, we miss opportunities to enhance productivity and retain great people. Too often we watch employees perform their jobs well, but fail to comment. Yet, the moment employees fall short of our expectations, we give them our full attention and plenty of advice. Such "red-pencil mentality" imitates an educational system that emphasizes errors by marking them in bright red. Correct answers, meanwhile, go unmarked—and seemingly unrecognized.

In business, we behave much the same way: We tend to pay close attention to the negative and ignore the positive. We call employees into the office only when things have gone wrong. Is it any wonder that employees often view management as "the enemy?"

The composition of our workforce has changed and will continue to change dramatically over the next several years. For managers interested in retaining employees and getting the best performance from them in the Future Workforce, the significance of employee recognition will be profound. New entrants into the workforce are of a generation that demands continual feedback, instant recognition, and diverse forms of recognition. They are demanding credit for, and acknowledgment of, their participation and ideas; they are neither interested in, nor willing to wait around for, five- and ten-year service awards. They come from a generation of self-preservation and self-concern and want to know WIIFM: **What's In It For Me?** Are you ready to give them an answer?

In my research, I found that the *#1 Excuse* managers offer for not recognizing their employees is, *"I don't have money in my budget for recognition,"* indicating they don't understand that there's a difference between recognition and reward. The *#2 Excuse* is *"I don't know how."* I've designed this book as a quick-reference management tool to eliminate these excuses, and to help you easily incorporate recognition into your daily management practice.

In the pages that follow, I've compiled a variety of practical, no-cost, ready-to-use ideas for how, when, and where you can demonstrate appreciation for the people you work with. The techniques in this book are proven. They're based on the responses and suggestions of the more than 25,000 employees I've researched and taught over the past six years—employees from all sectors of the world of work: nonprofit, small business, government, healthcare, and Fortune 500.

Recognizing and appreciating employees is not a remedy for poor management–employee relations, but it is a large part of establishing an organizational culture that gets "high marks." Ideally, demonstrating effective recognition should be a key competency for which managers are responsible and held accountable, along with financial planning, managing processes, and overseeing day-to-day operations. Minimally, it is a skill that all managers should seek to develop, because it is one of their most effective motivational tools.

This book is an important step toward making you a *great* manager, not just a good one. I hope you enjoy the journey!

—*Rosalind Jeffries*

*As simple as they are, saying thank-you
and giving praise are the most neglected forms
of recognition in the workplace.*

*For every employee who can't remember
the last time you heard a simple
"Thanks for a job well done,"
I'm telling you,
"Thanks for a job well done!"*

PART I:

The Who, What, and Why
of Recognition

What Are We *Really* Talking About?

It's a rare individual who doesn't derive satisfaction from being recognized for a job well done. Put another way, we're all suckers for attention. But the exciting news here is that the right kind of attention can do more than just make us feel good about ourselves and our efforts. For organizations seeking to maintain and strengthen employee morale—and at the same time boost productivity and innovation—the right kind of attention can be a powerful motivating tool.

So what exactly is the "right" kind of attention? This may come as a surprise. It is not necessarily money or material rewards. In fact, organizations are discovering that traditional and costly workforce motivators, such as promotions, salary increases, bonuses, certificates, gold watches, and the like, do not have the same impact they once did.

Times have changed, and so have today's workers. Whereas in years gone by, people began their careers expecting to remain loyal to one employer, workers in this new generation believe they will have multiple employers during their professional lives. In other words, they have different priorities. They don't work for the organization; they work for themselves. And, while they certainly are interested in earning a fair salary and traditional benefits, today's workers have additional standards by which they rate their jobs:

- They are looking for ways to balance the challenges of work and home.

- They want work that provides them with opportunities for professional and personal growth.

- They want their work to be meaningful.

- And they want to feel as though their good ideas and deeds are valued.

What can you do to let employees know that their efforts are appreciated? How do you show them that you are aware of their priorities? It's deceptively simple: You recognize them, their ideas, their accomplishments, and their efforts. Recognition is not only the right kind of attention, it's also a powerful motivator. And it goes hand in hand with appreciation and thank-you's.

Through recognition, you show your workers that you value them, that you appreciate the jobs they are doing, and that you care about their well-being. Recognition also helps people measure their performance. Unlike compensation—an expected element—recognition is special, and can leave a

Employees' Definition of Recognition:

"A response from someone that makes me feel good about what I am doing, have done, or will do."

lasting impression. Through a program of providing recognition on a personal, day-to-day basis, organizations can develop workers who have high self-esteem. There is ample research showing that confident workers are more productive, responsible, and creative. And, recognition costs little to nothing at all!

It's important to take a moment to examine the distinction between recognition and reward. A reward consists of money or something of financial value. Rewards are tangible. Recognition, on the other hand, is intangible, and may or may not be accompanied by a reward. It has been defined as "the act of acknowledging, approving, or appreciating an activity or service."

"When people believe in themselves they can accomplish anything."
—Stedman Graham
YOU CAN MAKE IT HAPPEN

Recognition is a vital method for acknowledging the importance of an individual's or team's contributions to the organization.

Given the tremendous advantages of recognition, you might think that most organizations would rely on it to motivate their workers. Think again. According to qualitative research conducted with more than 10,000 employees, 70 percent—that's 7 out of 10—of those surveyed said they would like more specific day-to-day recognition of their contributions. People are starving for attention!

Qualitative research showed that 7 out of 10 employees at all levels said they wanted specific individual recognition for a job well done.

More and more, human behavior professionals, management consultants, and others have come to focus on the importance of recognition in the workplace. This heightened attention has resulted in more organizations understanding the "what" and the "why" of recognition.

But many are still unsure of the "how." That is, how can organizations incorporate recognition into the daily management function? *101 Recognition Secrets* has the answers—valuable suggestions and strategies for using recognition effectively to motivate employees.

Clearly, recognition is worth doing—and it's worth doing right. It's not a quick-fix gimmick. Managers must be willing to make a long-term commitment to providing employees with personal recognition on an ongoing basis. Organizations that ignore the new employee values and the realities of the modern employment relationship will have a tough time improving morale, attracting and retaining top-quality employees, and staying competitive in the marketplace.

Here's Why It's So Important...

Providing effective recognition to employees is critical in today's business climate. Here's why:

- Reduced staffing levels require employees to assume more responsibility.

- Employees want to help shape a work life that is purposeful and motivating.

- In uncertain financial times, recognition provides an effective, low-cost way of encouraging higher levels of performance.

- Studies show that personal recognition is the most effective method of motivating staff.

- Recognition is an avenue to boost employee moral and respond to an employee's need for approval and acceptance.

- Recognition provides the means to make people feel valued in uncertain, changing times.

- Lack of recognition or appreciation is one of the most significant reasons employees leave their jobs.

- Research shows that there is a direct correlation between recognition and:

  - Meaningful work

  - Employee satisfaction

  - Productivity

  - Retention.

And Here's Why It's Going To Be
Even More Important...

The need for effective recognition as a retention tool already exists. It will become an even more critical management competency as significant changes occur in the workplace over the next several years.

- The Bureau of Labor Statistics projects that by 2010 there will be over 57 million job openings in the United States as a result of new jobs being created and existing jobs being vacated.

- Only about 29 million employees will be available to fill these positions.

- That means there could be a shortage of over 28 million workers within the next half-dozen years!

At the same time, the face of the workforce is changing dramatically. The Future Workforce will be characterized by:

- Greater diversity, as more women and minorities continue to enter the workplace.

- A shifting generational mix and wider generation gaps.

- Reduced employee loyalty and increased self-preservation.

- Employees saying, "I am unique. I want my own Employment Deal."

- New employment options targeting top talent.

Organizations that do not teach their managers how to respect, recognize, and value their employees will not be able to compete for top talent.

"Steady Eddies": The Forgotten 90%

Who deserves recognition? Everyone!

- Of our entire workforce, only about 5% are "superstars." These are the employees we generally think of when we think about recognition. And they are the employees who are certainly the easiest to recognize.

- At the other end of the spectrum, we have another 5% who are, perhaps, closer to fallen stars—our "problem children." These are the employees we spend a lot of time and energy on, typically in a negative or disciplinary way. But these marginal performers need recognition, too! You'll see more about that later in the book.

- And what about the other 90%, the average performers and "Steady Eddies" who come to work, do their jobs and then go home? The ones who are essentially invisible—and forgotten when it comes to recognition—because, *"They're not doing anything special. They're just doing their jobs."*

Think about it: What would happen to your department if they *didn't* come to work every day and do their assignments?

- Your "Steady Eddies" are the employees who row steadily, who keep your department afloat and on course every day.

- This group of employees is where you should be spending most of your recognition efforts, because this is where you have the greatest potential for increased productivity.

- Imagine what your work group could accomplish if 90% of them tried just a little harder every day because they knew that what they did mattered and was appreciated!

Good managers recognize their top performers, but...

Great managers recognize everyone!

Redefining Recognition

Recognition is about saying "thank-you" and making our employees feel appreciated. It is also about a whole lot more.

As the workforce changes and the competition for talented workers heats up, recognition must be redefined to include providing *all* our employees with:

- Meaningful and challenging work

- Career growth

- Learning and development

- Leadership.

This means that great managers and leaders are going to have to learn more about their employees than ever before. They are going to have to *invest in relationships*.

To be great managers, we must learn:

- To ask our employees what's important to *them*.

- How to determine what is important to each and every employee.

- New ways to recognize employee contributions.

- To ensure that diverse work motivators all have a place.

> *"Business is simple. Use the brains of your workers. Find the best ideas, inside and outside the company, and then put those ideas into practice. Recognize them with thank you's every step of the way."*
>
> —*Jack Welch*
> *Former CEO, General Electric*

PART II:

The How of Recognition

Characteristics of Effective Recognition

Relevant: Make sure that recognition is linked to performance!

Timely: Recognition should be given to an individual as soon as possible after the performance takes place. While immediate recognition is best, a good gauge is within 48 hours of the performance. Passage of time reduces the effectiveness of recognition.

Proportional: Don't overdo your recognition for "small stuff." This will make people question your motives. All good performance should be recognized, but in varying degrees.

Sincere: Insincere recognition is meaningless and can do great harm. Your employees know you better than you think. Be honest and open with them, and let them know you really appreciate their efforts.

Specific: An employee should be recognized for a specific behavior. To merely say "good job" isn't enough. Specific appreciation, such as, "The level of detail you added to the report was extremely useful in making key decisions," avoids the appearance of favoritism and cues the employee on what behavior should be repeated in the future.

Individualized: One size does not fit all; it only fits "one." Make your recognition fit the style of the individual being honored. How will you know you are using the right style? You will if you have asked employees what's important to _them_.

All individuals are different. Some individuals like public praise, while others prefer a private discussion. The best way of capturing employees' desires is to simply ask.

How to Use this Collection

This collection is packed with "how-to's" and things to remember. In fact, there's so much good information that it might be difficult figuring out how to use it all. Here are a few suggestions to get you started:

Keep Track of Your Favorite Secrets:

1. Read the following secrets from cover to cover with a highlighter in hand. Mark any key words or phrases that you find relevant and meaningful.

2. Make a to-do list of your favorite secrets.

3. Highlight what is important to you.

4. Have a bookmark available to mark where you left off.

5. Dog-ear the page corners.

6. Put red Post-it® Flags on your hot choices.

7. Think of individuals you work with every day who are deserving of something you highlighted. Make a decision to acknowledge those individuals within the next three days.

8. Create a STAR Report. Identify the **S**pecific **T**ask, **A**ction Taken, and **R**ecognition given for each individual on your team.

Get Your Employees Involved:

9. Have employees pretend they are ON THE RADIO.

   On a flip chart, draw a large radio with the dial set to **WIIFM** (**W**hat's **I**n **I**t **F**or **M**e).

Divide the employees into small groups. Instruct them to develop a mock radio broadcast segment (news bulletin, public service announcement, interview, etc.) that explains what's in it for all employees to recognize peers and bosses (that is, how they benefit when they recognize someone else). This will help establish a culture of recognition within your department, making it more than a one-person show.

Discuss the Experience, Results and Key Learning:

10. Have employees read the secrets and select their top three and what behaviors they demonstrate that are worthy of recognition.

11. Use green Post-it® Flags for employee choices.

Here They Are!
101 Recognition Secrets

Here are some ideas for little things that make a big difference! Try these "secrets" or your own variations to let your employees know you appreciate their work. As you read these secrets or think about your own, remember:

To say "Thank-You" also means to:

- Acknowledge

- Appreciate

- Pay tribute

- Laud

- RECOGNIZE!

Thank-You
"A really neglected form of compensation."
—*Robert Townsend*
Actor

1. Special Committee Assignment

Selecting an employee for a special committee assignment tells them that you trust them and that their opinions count! The message to the employee is that they are important and can handle "special assignments."

2. Design a Thermometer

Any goal seems more attainable when you can see it and map your progress. Be sure to celebrate milestones along the way. Think of the excitement as the temperature rises!

3. Establish a Monthly "Learning Exchange"

This opportunity will promote teamwork and is a no-cost educational opportunity for managers *and* employees to share what they have recently learned or found interesting.

4. Allow Employees to Make Decisions about Things Affecting Their Work

Allowing employees to make their own decisions empowers them, promotes accountability, and teaches prioritization.

"There are many ways to honor someone. Just doing it is an asset."

—SUCCESSFUL MEETINGS MAGAZINE

5. Allow Room for Stretch Assignments

Stretching your mind is as necessary as stretching your body. It promotes flexibility, creativity, and overall good health. Keep employees from becoming bored and mentally stiff. Provide challenging work to let them know you see them as competent and empowered.

6. Explain WHY We Do Things

Explaining *why* provides a better understanding of *how*—just what your employees need to perform even better!

"At the heart of effective leadership is genuinely caring for people."

—*Kouzes/Posner*
ENCOURAGING THE
HEART

7. Certificate of Achievement

Frame it to make it even more special and more likely to be displayed. A certificate provides validation of a job well done—something accomplished—and putting it on paper creates a lasting impression.

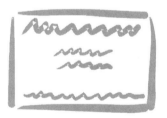

8. Trip to a Supplier Site

A trip away from the office, especially for a member of the support staff, can mean as much as a day of vacation. Employees will not only feel extra special, they will also begin to understand the impact of what they do and how they fit into the bigger picture.

"What makes workers tick? Lots of things, but high on the list are variety, recognition and fun."

—Amy Joyce
THE WASHINGTON POST

9. Special Tools or Resources

Providing special chairs or upgrading software increases workplace satisfaction. By adding value for your employees, they add value to the bottom line.

10. Brag Time

Allow time during meetings for staff members to brag about the outstanding job a department employee did on a specific project. Make a meeting a celebration of performance.

11. Main Lobby Photo Displays

Feature outstanding work groups at your organization in a photo and write-up display in a highly visible place, such as the main lobby.

"To truly recognize someone in a special caring way, concentrate on that person as a unique individual."

—Barbara Glanz
Care Packages

12. Welcoming and Orienting New Employees

Develop alternative ideas for welcoming new employees to your department. For example, place a rose on the newcomer's desk, along with a card saying, "This bud's for you. Thanks for joining our team." In addition, make transition to the department easier for new employees by offering a creative orientation to the department that involves communication with others outside the department.

13. Birthday Mail

Have managers and employees sign a card and mail it to the honoree's house before the "big day" instead of presenting it at a monthly office birthday party.

14. A Special Invitation

Recognize employees by inviting them to receive specialized in-house training from upper management.

15. Business Cards

Every employee, from a member of the house-keeping staff to the highest paid executive, is responsible for the success of the business. Provide everyone with business cards to demonstrate that you value their contribution and professionalism.

16. Farewell Recognition

Take a moment to recognize every departing employee for their efforts while working in your organization.

"The deepest principle in human nature is the craving to be appreciated."
—William James
Philosopher

17. Employee of the Month News Release

Send a news release on your "Employee of the Month" to the employee's hometown newspaper.

18. Congratulatory Memo

Write your employee a personal note of congratulations for excellent performance on handling a difficult customer.

19. Kudos

"Kudo" means an award or honor, a compliment, or praise. Develop small but meaningful awards for your employees for doing something "great!" For example, give Kudos® candy bars for assisting a very difficult customer.

"Really seeking to understand another person is probably one of the most important deposits you can make, and it is the key to every other deposit."
—Steven Covey
THE 7 HABITS OF HIGHLY EFFECTIVE PEOPLE

20. Family Appreciation Letter

Send an appreciation letter to an employee's family, thanking family members for their understanding and support when the employee had to put in long hours of overtime.

21. Weekday Surprise

Surprise your staff with something nice on any day of the week for finishing a project, completing inventory, or meeting quotas, by having a stress-free activity. For example, invite your staff to have punch and cookies for 15 minutes to just relax.

22. Your Substitute

Ask employees to attend a meeting in your place when you are not available.

23. Random Acts of Kindness

Give recognition to employees who perform acts of kindness and other good deeds, both on the job and out in the world. When an employee stops to help an elderly person with a heavy package, or assist a stranded motorist, or does something else to help another human being, we all benefit.

24. Timely Feedback

Give your employees feedback—positive or negative—in a timely fashion.

"I'd give more praise."
— *The Duke of Wellington*
Victor at the Battle of
Waterloo

25. Mentor for Newcomers

Ask an employee to serve as a mentor for a new employee.

26. Meet and Greet Those at the Top

Take time to introduce your employees to upper management so that effective team building and positive recognition can occur.

27. Attention for Efforts that Go Unnoticed

Plan ways to recognize hardworking employees whose efforts are often unseen because of infrequent contact with the public. For example, recognize your administrative assistant with a roll of Life Savers® for creating an easier filing system.

"No one rises to low expectations."

—Les Brown
COURAGE TO LIVE YOUR DREAMS

28. Take a Break With Employees

Have coffee or lunch with an employee or a group of employees you don't normally see every day.

29. Recognition Coffees

Take a short coffee break from a busy schedule to recognize and support an employee for a job well done.

30. Note Performance Improvements

Jot down a message to an employee on your personal stationery, recognizing him or her for better performance on the job.

31. Department-Based Publicity

Inform employees about upcoming events through fliers, table tent cards, and other methods.

32. Top Management Participation

Ask your boss to attend a meeting with your employees during which you recognize both individuals and groups for specific contributions.

33. Publicize Achievements

Make sure that department and employee achievements are recognized in your organization's newsletter.

34. Good News in Personnel Files

Send a letter of commendation to the personnel department for inclusion in an employee's personnel folder. And let the employee know you did this by sending them a note and a copy of the letter.

35. Appreciation Days

Gather your employees to plan a special appreciation day for your department or for certain employees who deserve recognition.

36. Training Policy

Create a department policy that at least 16 hours of professional development time per year will be made available for each employee.

37. Courtesy Time Off

Grant employees a day or two of leave for special or personal events in their lives.

"One of the top ten key drivers of employee engagement in the future is providing recognition to talented employees."

—Margaret Regan
FutureWork Institute

38. Year in Review

Produce a year-in-review booklet with pictures, or plan a celebration to highlight your employees' proudest achievements of the year.

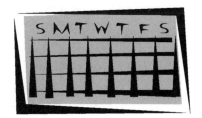

39. Understanding the "Big Picture"

Help your employees see and understand the "Big Picture." Arrange to have employees from your department visit another company work area they interface with. Allow the employees to plan the visit and explore how their product or service fits into the overall scheme of things.

40. Staff Development

Recognize and encourage your staff members by allowing them to attend workshops, seminars, and other functions. Give special assignments to people who have shown interest and initiative.

41. Monthly Talk Sessions

Energize your staff with monthly talk sessions. Allow approximately 20 minutes as an agenda item to have employees talk about what's going well, what's not going well, and what help they need from you.

"You never know when a moment and a few sincere words can have an impact on someone's life."

—*Zig Ziglar*
SEE YOU AT THE TOP

42. Accentuate the Positive

Tell people what they've done right—not just what they've done wrong—on an ongoing basis.

43. Growth Factors

Recognize an employee who has mastered a new skill or shown professional growth by giving him or her a plant.

44. Cross-Department Recognition

Contact another employee's supervisor to inform him or her of the employee's positive behavior and performance in your presence.

"We applaud each little success one after another and the first thing you know, they actually become successful. We praise them to success!"

—*Mary Kay Ash, CEO*
Mary Kay Cosmetics

45. Help Employees to Be in the Know

Share information from:

- Meetings you attend within the organization

- Journals you read

- Professional meetings you attend outside the organization.

46. Picture This

Involve employees in creating a logo or symbol that represents your department's work or contribution to the organization. This logo can be used on T-shirts, mugs, or memos, and in any departmental activity.

"We are all suckers for attention."

—*Susan Cook*
TURNED ON

47. Drumming Up Support

Recognize individuals who lead groups, projects, or exercises by making them "Honorary Drum Majors." Give each a baton to make the title complete.

"Positive reinforcement has to be a daily affair. No matter how much money or time you spend on rewards and recognition, you will not get the results you want if the organization gets things done with negative reinforcement day to day. As Tom Odom of Shell Oil says, 'It's hard to celebrate when you've been beat up on the way to the party.'"

—Aubrey Daniels
BRINGING OUT THE
BEST IN PEOPLE

48. Express Appreciation

- In words

- With a smile

49. Thanks for Working Overtime

Write a thank-you note to an employee for putting in extra time in the workplace.

50. Day-To-Day Thank-You's

Thank your employees frequently through letters, notes, or personal comments for something positive they've done.

51. Thanks to You, Boss

Express thanks to your manager when he or she has done something well or helpful to you.

52. Thank-You Boutonniere

Recognize an employee's positive performance and exemplary workplace behavior with a boutonniere or flower to brighten up his or her day.

53. Thank-You Goodie Baskets

Distribute a basket of candies or other goodies to employees in your department or section to show your appreciation for something specific they've done.

54. Employee-to-Employee Thank-You's

Visit a fellow employee personally, or send a note, saying thank-you for the help, or offering a kind word of encouragement.

55. Thank-You in Rough Times

Take a moment to personally thank your employees for a specific task completed during a period of heavy work.

57. Quality Efforts

Cite extraordinary efforts that result in quality performance, in the organization newsletter or on a bulletin board.

56. Team Day

Set aside a day for teams in cross-functional departments to present their results and processes to one another.

58. Seek Input

Ask employees for their ideas and feedback. Simply asking people for more input is a flattering form of recognition.

59. Certificates for Training

Present certificates to employees who successfully use—not just complete—training.

"Praising all alike is praising none."

—*John Gay*
Epistles

60. Grace Under Pressure

Recognize an employee who handles a stressful situation particularly well with a certificate or special award.

61. Building Bridges

Encourage staff members to recognize each other's contributions by verbally thanking one another and creating their own forms of recognition.

62. "Star" Performers

Feature an employee who has been an overall quality performer on the job in the organization newsletter.

63. Exemplary Customer Service

Recognize employees who demonstrate exemplary customer service through:

- A letter

- A lunch certificate

- A story about them in a newsletter

- Acknowledgment by upper management

- A gift certificate for a fun shopping spree.

*This is an opportunity for the customer service employee to **receive** customer service.*

64. Anniversary Date

Commemorate notable anniversaries of service (such as 5, 10, or 20 years), by sending the employee a card of congratulations.

65. Feedback From Boss

Tell employees when they've done a good job at the time of the event.

66. Rest Stop (or R&R)

Recognize an employee's hard work by presenting him or her with a pillow or a gift certificate for a massage.

"We blow up the most when we feel unappreciated."

—*Ava Fluty*
Career Track

67. International Day of Sharing

Recognize the many cultures and ethnic groups that employees of your organization represent by providing treats that are representative of their nationalities.

68. Recognition Week

Designate a week for recognizing employees for their hospitality and hard work through various activities and events.

69. Monthly Luncheon

Have monthly luncheons and invite guests from other departments to exchange ideas and views. This will help your staff gain appreciation for the work others do.

70. Say Hello, Always

Make a point of always saying "hello" to employees when you pass by their desk or pass them in the hall.

"Recognition for a job well done is the top motivator of employee performance."

—*Bob Nelson*
1001 WAYS TO REWARD EMPLOYEES

71. Hot Chocolate for Everyone

Warm up your employees and guests on a cold winter day with cups of hot chocolate.

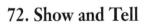

72. Show and Tell

Have employees develop presentations for other employees on "Here Is What I Do."

73. Managers Need Recognition, Too!

Recognition works at all levels. Senior management should recognize their direct reports who practice giving recognition to their employees. This is one way to emphasize the importance of recognition as a *Great Management Practice*.

"Employees want to contribute their gifts to people who appreciate them!"

—Michele Hunt
DREAM MAKERS: PUTTING VISION AND VALUES TO WORK

---

74. Popsicle® Day

Recognize employees for their hard work and dedication with a Popsicle® on a hot summer day.

"You have to be able to listen well if you're going to motivate the people who work for you."

—*Lee Iacocca*
Former CEO

75. "Welcome Back" Update

When employees return from vacation, welcome them back and bring them up to date.

76. Message Center

Designate a message center for all pertinent memos, letters, and information. The center can also serve as a place for staff to record ideas and information they want to share with one another.

77. Create an Award

Create a prestigious department award, such as a designer pen or plaque.

78. Employee of the Month

Develop an employee of the month program, with special recognition given by top management. Include special, creative, inexpensive gifts for the recognized employees.

79. Interior Design

Get employees involved in decorating their offices/work areas to help create a feeling of personal pride and ownership.

"People work for money but go the extra mile for recognition, praise and rewards."

—Stuart Levine
Former CEO, Dale Carnegie

80. Department of the Year

Choose a department of the year based on guidelines you establish.

"Everyone needs recognition. It helps people measure their performance."

—*Rita Maehling*
RECOGNITION REDEFINED

81. Employee Involvement

Ask your employees how you can best show your appreciation. What recognition would they like from you?

82. Appreciation Sound-Off

Invite an individual into your office for 10 minutes specifically to acknowledge their accomplishment. Make sure the appreciation gesture is genuine and specific.

83. Walking Rounds

Go to your employees instead of them always coming to you. Take "walking rounds" to visit employees at their work sites. This gives you an opportunity to receive feedback on how their jobs are going and to compliment them on their work environment.

"What really flatters a man is that you think him worth flattering."

—*George Bernard Shaw*
Playwright

84. Recognition of Special Events

Make special mention of important personal employee events, such as a marriage, graduation, or birth of a child.

85. Call People by Name

Whenever possible, call a person by name. It has been said that the most welcome word in the English language to each individual is his or her name.

86. Honor Roll

Create an honor roll of employees recognized by clients, suppliers, and others for their acts of kindness and support on the job.

87. Recognition at Meetings

Have well-planned meetings:

- Recognize employees by asking them to plan and conduct a meeting.

- Ensure that any recognition ceremony at a meeting is carefully prepared and thoughtfully presented.

88. Wish List

Have employees complete a wish list of ideas they believe would benefit the department and organization. Implement ideas that are effective and reasonable.

89. Pictures

Frame pictures of employees and place them prominently on a wall in their department.

90. Community Ties

Create a community service award to be publicized in the local paper as well as internally within the organization.

"The single biggest complaint American workers have about their managers is feeling unappreciated.

—Franklin Ashby
EMBRACING EXCELLENCE

91. Support Staff Recognition

Create an award to recognize individuals who are not in the limelight, but without whose help a product or project could not have been accomplished.

92. Grand Plans

Present an employee with a $100 Grand® candy bar in recognition of a "grand" idea.

93. Great Beginnings

Briefly attend the first
meeting of a quality
improvement team to
express your appreciation to
members for their
involvement.

94. Thank-You's from Higher-Ups

Invite the appropriate senior
level administrator to attend
a department meeting to
thank employees for their
contributions to a
department achievement.

95. Sensitivity

Take time to get to know
each of your employees
informally so you are
sensitive to their unique
needs and can recognize
individuals in ways that meet
those needs.

*"No act of kindness, no matter
how small, is ever wasted."*
— *AESOP'S FABLES*

96. Employee Lounges

Establish a comfortable and appealing area within the department where employees can go when taking a break.

97. Thank-You's at Project Conclusion

Send a letter to every team member at the conclusion of their work on a project, thanking each for his or her contribution.

98. Ambassador of the Quarter

Have employees choose an ambassador of the quarter as a method to recognize those who display exemplary performance.

"Employees want to do a good job; if they are provided the proper environment, they will do so."

—*Kathryn Wall*
THE HEALTHCARE
TRAINING HANDBOOK

99. Credit When Credit Is Due

Remember to give credit to those who have introduced great ideas and completed special projects.

"Giving people a chance to be 'visible' for their work and accomplishments is the smartest thing a manager can do to motivate them."

— BITS AND PIECES

100. Flexibility in Schedules

Allow employees to work a flexible schedule while still maintaining the normal number of work hours.

101. Department Newsletter

Establish a newsletter in your department to inform your employees of current events within the organization.

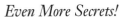

Even More Secrets!

102. Become a Working Member

Spend a day "in the trenches," working "hands on" with the employees in your department.

103. Go Out of Your Way to Recognize Employees

Make a special trip to an employee's office to express appreciation for a job well done.

104. Community Involvement

As a department or on behalf of a particular employee, make a donation to a favorite charity. This strengthens staff unity and shows community involvement.

"Personal recognition remains as one of the most important elements leading to high motivation."

—Gregory Smith
THE NEW LEADER

105. Bright Ideas

Encourage employees to present their own ideas or program possibilities to management.

106. Offsite Meetings

Schedule meeting days off site to provide employees with the opportunity to plan in a different environment. This will give employees further opportunity to contribute to the overall goals of the department.

107. Bulletin Board

Construct a bulletin board for your department to display such items as letters, memos, pictures, and thank-you cards that recognize employees.

"When you are looking for obstacles, you can't find opportunities."
—*Janet Cheatham Bell*
Famous Black Quotations

108. Traveling Trophy

Purchase a trophy that travels each month to the department exhibiting the greatest overall performance —behaviors *and* results— throughout the organization during the previous month.

109. The Envelope, Please

Draft a thank-you letter to be signed by the next level of management or, when appropriate, by the vice president or general manager.

110. Highlights

Create a department newsletter that recognizes employees for their humanistic actions and behaviors.

111. Policy Changes

Allow your employees to participate in forming or changing policies that affect the department.

"The manner in which the gift is given is worth more than the gift."

—Anonymous

112. Enter-prize

Establish a suggestion program that recognizes employees for their creative ideas regarding cost containment and improved operations.

Special Cases:
A Word or Two about...

Recognizing Geographically Dispersed Work Groups

Recognizing and motivating members of a geographically dispersed work group is a particularly difficult—and increasingly common—challenge. Making these individuals feel as though they are an integral part of your department or organization is a critical part of making them feel valued.

- Send a handwritten note card (delivered by courier or overnight delivery service, if possible) acknowledging their specific contribution.

- Don't assume that organization-wide policies will work for dispersed work groups. Ask for their input, and be flexible.

- Make sure they have a "space of their own" to work in when visiting the home office.

- Make sure they have an opportunity to participate in organization-wide celebrations and meetings.

Recognizing Bosses and Coworkers

Once you start, recognition becomes a way of life—a way of interacting with people, whether or not they work for you. Peer recognition lets the people you work with know they are appreciated for the little things they do, as well as for the big things.

- Recognize your boss.

- Recognize your coworkers.

- Recognize individuals in the organization who don't work for you but with whom you interact.

While you are not responsible for how well these individuals perform their jobs, you can recognize their contributions to the organization in general, or your department in particular. Peer recognition is one of the most effective ways of building good working relationships.

Even if these people never recognize you, set the example!

Recognizing the Different Generations

With four generations in the workplace for the first time in the history of the United States, recognition has become even more of a challenge, because what we value depends on when and how we grew up.

The following suggestions for recognizing individuals across the four generations are based on what we know about the general characteristics of each generation. But be careful! Every individual is different. These ideas are only meant to give you a starting place.

To recognize *Traditionalists* (*born 1922–1943*):

- Take time for the personal touch. Handwrite a note rather than using email.

- Let them have the flexibility to socialize and chat with coworkers between assignments.

- Honor their hard work with plaques and other symbolic records of achievement.

To recognize *Baby Boomers* (*born 1943–1960*):

- Give them lots of public recognition.

- Give them a chance to prove themselves and their worth.

- Give them perks with status.

- Ask for their input and get their consensus.

- Help them gain name recognition.

- Reward their work ethic and long hours.

To recognize *Generation X-ers* (*born 1960–1980*):

- Give them lots of projects to control and prioritize.

- Give them constant feedback.

- Give them time to pursue other interests and have fun at work.

- Invest in the latest technology.

- Be conscious of perks up the ladder. X-ers don't crave status symbols, but they can be resentful when others get them.

To recognize *Generation Y-ers* (*born after 1980*):

- Learn about their personal goals and link them to the organization's.

- Make all opportunities truly equal—forget about traditional gender roles.

- Open avenues for education and skill-building.

- Establish a mentor program.

Recognizing Marginal Performers

Ask yourself:

- Why is this employee a marginal performer?

- What can I do to improve their performance?

- How can I provide recognition?

Ask the employee:

- What do you like about what you did?

- What would you do differently if you could ?

- What help do you need from me?

- What is "success" to you?

Typical causes of marginal performance are:

- Lack of clarity regarding desired performance.

- Employee is not challenged.

- Personal problems.

- Lack of proper orientation to the job.

- Substance abuse.

- Lack of adequate skills.

- Wrong "hire" for the job.

Tips for Working with Marginal Employees:

- Remember that every person has different wants, needs, and expectations.

- Assess each situation individually and act accordingly.

- Provide specific training.

- Redefine the job.

- Seek assistance through the Employee Assistance Program (EAP).

- Perform a skills assessment.

- Provide career development/planning.

- Provide opportunity for growth.

- Ask for the employee's input.

- Involve the employee in decision-making.

- Notice and acknowledge positive behavior.

20 Ways to Get Rid of Your Employees

Do you ever wonder why your employees quit? Employees have said it's because their bosses:

1. **NEVER** ask, "What do you think?"

2. **NEVER** say, "Thanks."

3. **NEVER** take time to listen.

4. **NEVER** allow the "F" word (fun) to happen.

5. **NEVER** keep them informed.

6. **NEVER** allow room for new ideas.

7. **NEVER** change job routine.

8. **NEVER** have staff meetings.

9. **NEVER** have conferences except for evaluation purposes.

10. **NEVER** show empathy.

11. NEVER
acknowledge an employee's strengths.

12. NEVER
ask employees about their personal goals.

13. NEVER
make a person feel "special."

14. NEVER
notice consistent performers.

15. NEVER
get employee commitment.

16. NEVER
acknowledge a job well done.

17. NEVER
allow for learning and development.

18. NEVER
give credit when credit is due to an individual.

19. NEVER
bother to say, "Good morning."

20. NEVER
ask for input when decisions are being made.

PART III:

A Practitioner's Guide— Four Steps to Effective Recognition

Step 1: Ask Your Employees!
Find Out What *They* Really Want

The best way to find out what employees really want is to ask them! Begin to build a database for each of your employees. The information for your database will come directly from having each of your employees do the exercises and answer the questions on the next few pages.

Pay special attention to the sample employee responses that are included. They are real-life examples, and they might surprise you! They're included to give you an idea of the type of things your own employees might say, and to offer you a variety of ideas about how to tailor your own recognition strategy.

These four exercises can be lots of fun. By simply asking these questions, you're beginning the process of individualized recognition!

Exercise 1: Exploring "Missed Opportunities"

This is a great exercise you can use to find out what's really important to your employees. Ask them the two questions below and have them write their answers on a flip chart.

✔ *When should you have been recognized and it didn't happen?*

✔ *What would you have liked to have happen?*

The information you get back is very powerful because it not only gives you insight into *what they believe deserves recognition*, but also gives examples of *how they would like to be recognized.*

Q: List a time when you or someone you know should have been recognized and it didn't happen?	Q: What would you have liked to have happen?
"I worked successfully on a project for six months, but received no recognition when I presented it. My supervisor just took the report without even thanking me."	"A simple thanks and an acknowledgment in front of my peers."
"When I first started working here, nobody welcomed me or introduced me to other employees. I felt invisible!"	"I would have liked for the other employees to know in advance that I would be joining the team. Maybe coffee with the group for about 10 minutes."

Q: *List a time when you or someone you know should have been recognized and it didn't happen?*	Q: *What would you have liked to have happen?*
"The computer system I designed and set up for our department is running great. But the manager hasn't even said 'thank-you!'"	"Just a verbal compliment would have been nice."
"Michael Jordan's last home game with the Washington WIZARDS went virtually unnoticed. There was no fanfare—it was a quiet, simplistic sendoff."	The fans were outraged! They thought Michael should have gotten a lot more verbal thank-you's. As Washington, D.C. DJ Donnie Simpson said, 'It wouldn't have cost anything to really say, 'Thank you, Michael.'"

Exercise 2: What Makes a Boss Great?

Ask your employees to complete the following:

✔ *Tell me one thing a former boss did that made you feel valued and appreciated.*

Once again, their answers will give you insight into the types of recognition that are meaningful to your own employees. Common responses are:

- "Explained" why we did things.

- Told me she had confidence in my skills.

- Gave me challenging projects and encouraged risk taking.

- Involved me in decisions.

- Honesty—he told the staff how it was.

- Took time to listen.

- Showed confidence in me by not micromanaging.

Exercise 3: Link Recognition to Goals and Outcomes

Have your employees review the goals, values, and products of your work group. Then ask them to make a list of the *behaviors, efforts, and outcomes* that they think deserve recognition. Have them write their ideas in the left-hand column titled, "What Deserves Recognition," as shown below. Ask them to write examples of how they would like to be recognized for each of these ideas in the right-hand column.

Q: What deserves recognition?	*Q. How would you like to receive recognition?*
Sacrificing personal time	A simple "thanks"
Attention to detail	A fine-point pen

Q: *What deserves recognition?*	Q. *How would you like to receive recognition?*
Dealing with difficult situations.	A nice stress reliever foam ball to squeeze away the tension.
Consistently taking on new projects.	Give me credit and be my mentor to help me grow in my job.
Customer satisfaction—anticipating what the customer needs.	Allow me to mentor others.
Consistently performing good work	A book by a favorite author with a note card.

Wow! Just look at the type of data you get!

Exercise 4: Find Out What They Don't Like

Because we're all different, it's sometimes just as important to find out how employees don't like to be recognized. So be sure to ask them the following question:

✔ *How do you **not** wish to be recognized?*

Once again, answers to this question will give you a unique perspective of what your employees value. Common responses are:

- Don't use sarcasm, or unflattering or humorous awards.

- Don't wait until evaluation time.

- Don't wait until a long time after the event.

- Don't send me a form letter.

- Don't use vague statements like "good job."

Step 2: Listen with a Fresh Ear!
Phrases to Rephrase

To be effective, recognition needs to be individualized and specific. All too often, we think we are doing a good job of giving recognition, but in reality we are being too vague or generic for our words to be meaningful to our employees.

Learn to listen to yourself with a fresh set of ears, asking: *Am I really making meaningful, specific statements of appreciation?*

Take a look at the examples on the following pages to see how you can turn vague comments into meaningful statements of recognition.

Vague or Generic Comments	*Meaningful, Specific Statements*
Great job!	Gina, I really appreciate the fact that you paid specific attention to line #9 in the billing application. It brought us an additional $20,000 in savings this year.
You're really a lifesaver!	Jim, I really appreciate how you jumped in to cover the phones today so that Jenny could take care of an unexpected task. Because of you, our customers received great service!

Vague or Generic Comments	*Meaningful, Specific Statements*
Keep up the good work!	Thanks, Fred, for taking the initiative to make arrangements for the office move. Your attention to the packing, carpet selection, and follow-up with suppliers was critical to a smooth remodeling of the office.
Thanks for your help!	Nancy, your idea for figuring out our vacation schedule was brilliant! Thanks to your suggestion, everyone has an opportunity to get the dates they want without feeling there is any favoritism.

Step 3: Plan and Practice!
Use this Four-Step Planning Sheet

When you first begin actively recognizing employees, it requires a bit of planning… and lots of practice. Eventually, however, it will become like breathing: You won't even notice you're doing it! That's when you know you've moved up from being a good boss to being a great boss!

The payoffs to planning and practice are tremendous: Every employee will feel respected for his or her contribution; you will see an increase in productivity; and your department will see an immediate, positive impact on employee retention and morale.

Until that happens, try this: Identify the person or team you would like to recognize. Then review the four-step planning sheet on the next page for each person or team.

Four-Step Planning Sheet

Name: _____

1. Describe in detail which behavior(s) you want to acknowledge.

2. How does this behavior affect the person or team, the department, and the organization?

3. Where will the recognition activity or celebration take place?

4. What words will you use to express appreciation for the specific behavior(s) described above?

Step 4: Remember the Basics!
A Final Word about Recognition Essentials

In today's world of work, it's easy to become distracted and to forget about recognition. Until recognizing your employees becomes second nature, try making a copy of these recognition essentials and keeping it where you will see it often.

Remember:

The most desired form of recognition is a simple, genuine, specific, spoken or written "Thank-You!"

Giving meaningful recognition takes only a few minutes of your time.

Recognition must be tailored to the individual; one size does not fit all.

Asking your employees what deserves recognition is vital, because it enables you to provide unique and effective recognition tailored to the person.

It's important to pay close attention to the special recognition needs of shy and private people.

Incorporating positive recognition may require a change in your management style.

Practice makes giving recognition easier.

Watching and listening to how others give recognition is an excellent way to learn what's important to *them*.

Sample Worksheets for Data Gathering

ASK—You don't have to wonder!

On the following pages are sample exercises you can use with your staff. Your answers will become a "database" you can use to store information on every employee in your department. For information on completing these exercises, refer to pages 94–102.

Remember, the best way to find out what employees really want is to ASK THEM!

Exploring Missed Opportunities with Your Employees

What Makes a Boss Great?

What Deserves Recognition?

How Would You Like to Receive Recognition?

How Do You Not Wish to be Recognized?

Recognition Notes

Recognition Notes

Recognition Notes

Recognition Notes

Acknowledgments

A very special and heartfelt thanks to my friend and collaborator, Regina Guaraldi, for listening day after day to my stories and my constant frustration that "managers still don't know how important this is!"

Thanks to Nancy McKeithen, my dream editor, who understood and believed in this book—and who did all the right things with it to make it come to life.

Special thanks to Performance Technology, Inc., for their expertise and assistance in gathering and analyzing data, and to "the Colonel," both for sharing with us the unsurpassed recognition "secrets" of the U.S. Army, and for always urging us onward.

Thank-you to Erica Holloway for her unfailing sense of humor and for sharing her "30-something" perspective.

Thanks to my publicist, Linda Lazar Allen, for her insight, direction, and encouragement every step of the way.

Appreciation also to Kevin O'Sullivan for his thoughtful suggestions prior to printing of this latest edition.

I thank my mother, a true Southerner, who couldn't believe that you actually have to teach people how important it is to say "thank-you." Thanks, Mom, for your wisdom and for instilling in me to "be the best I can be and someone will notice."

Finally, thanks to my family, and especially my daughter, Ashley, for understanding all the times I couldn't be there because I was traveling to conduct the research for this book.

About the Author

Rosalind (Roz) Jeffries was the first to research the topic of recognition in the healthcare industry in the early 1980s. Ms. Jeffries is the president of Performance Enhancement Group, Inc., a consulting and training company. Her first book, ***101 Recognition Secrets: Tools for Motivating Today's Workforce***, is being used in many organizations throughout the world. Her strategies, workshops, and systems deliver an increase in retention, and her real-world tools show ways to tie recognition into everyday life.

Bringing over 25 years of experience in the training and organization development profession as an internal and external practitioner, Ms. Jeffries offers unsurpassed expertise and perspective. Her book and workshops are based on the results of a six-year project examining the power of recognition with over 25,000 managers and employees in organizations of all types and sizes, from small businesses to government agencies to Fortune 500 companies. Through interviews, workshops, focus groups, and chat rooms online, Ms. Jeffries has identified the most effective (and ineffective) forms of recognition for organizations.

To order additional copies of *101 Recognition Secrets* or receive additional information on Recognition Training Workshops, please contact:

Performance Enhancement Group
Bethesda, MD

Ph: 301-656-4600
Fax: 301-656-4625

www.recognitionsecrets.com